Sir Charles Tupper

The bully who battled for Canada

Written by Johanna Bertin
Illustrated by Gabriel Morrissette and Bernie Mireault

D1273751

Photo Credits
JackFruit Press Ltd. would like to thank Library and Archives Canada for images appearing on pages 29 (C-000733), 39 (E-007140520 and PA-182804), and 55 (C-000733).

© 2007 JackFruit Press Ltd.
Publisher and Editor— Jacqueline Brown
Designer and Art Director — Marcel Lafleur
Researchers — Barbara Baillargeon and Hagit Hadaya

All rights reserved. No part of this book may be reproduced, stored in a retrieval system, or transmitted, in any form or by any means, without the prior written permission of JackFruit Press Ltd. or, in the case of photocopying or other reprographic copying, a licence from The Canadian Copyright Licensing Agency (Access Copyright).

For an Access Copyright licence, visit www.accesscopyright.ca or call (toll-free) 1-800-893-5777.

JackFruit Press Ltd.
Toronto, Canada
www.jackfruitpress.com

Library and Archives Canada Cataloguing in Publication

Bertin, Johanna
Sir Charles Tupper: The bully who battled for Canada / written by Johanna Bertin; illustrated by Gabriel Morrissette and Bernie Mireault.

(Canadian prime ministers: warts and all #6)
Includes index.
ISBN 978-0-9736406-7-0

1. Tupper, Charles, Sir, 1821–1915—Juvenile literature. 2. Prime ministers—Canada—Biography—Juvenile literature. 3. Prime ministers—Nova Scotia—Biography—Juvenile literature. 4. Canada—Politics and government—1867–1896—Juvenile literature. 5. Nova Scotia—Politics and government—19th century—Juvenile literature. 6. Physicians—Canada—Biography—Juvenile literature. I. Gabriel Morrissette and Bernie Mireault, 1959–   , 1961–   . II. Title. III. Series.

FC526.T8B47 2006   j971.05'5092
C2006-903403-6

Printed and bound in India

...So, I'm here to show you around this really cool series of books on great Canadians.

This book tells the story of Sir Charles Tupper, Canada's sixth prime minister.

Some people thought Charles was a bully, because when he got a good idea, he was determined to make it a reality!

Contents

Hot topics

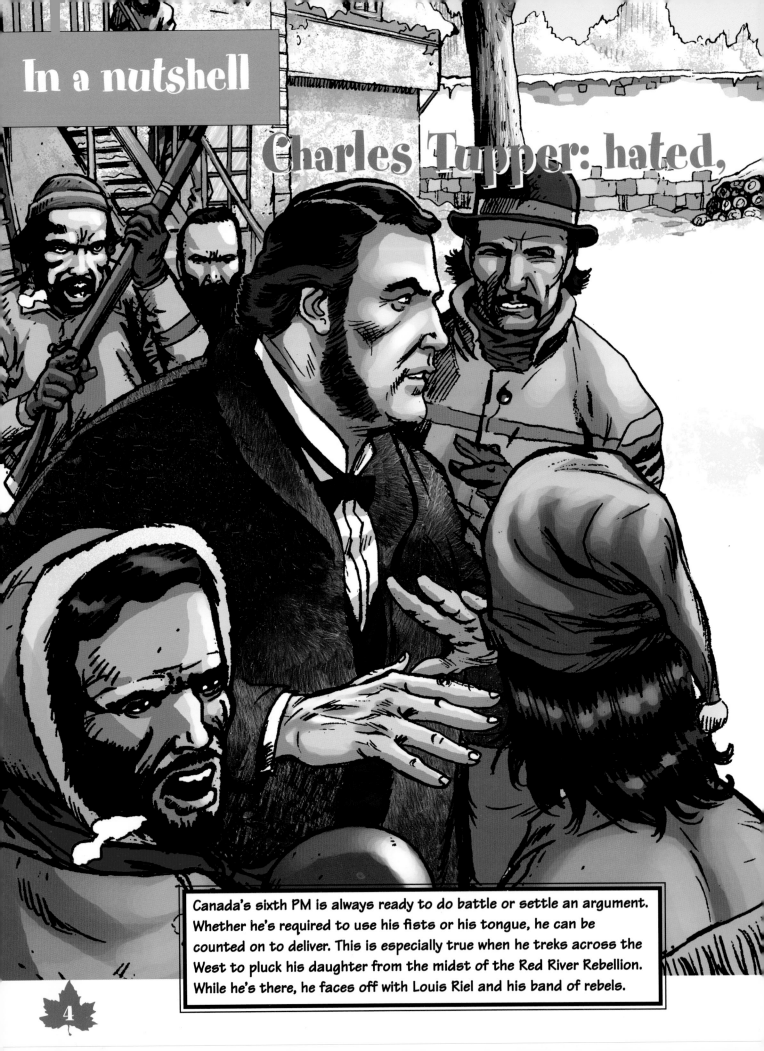

In a nutshell

Charles Tupper: hated,

Canada's sixth PM is always ready to do battle or settle an argument. Whether he's required to use his fists or his tongue, he can be counted on to deliver. This is especially true when he treks across the West to pluck his daughter from the midst of the Red River Rebellion. While he's there, he faces off with Louis Riel and his band of rebels.

knighted, despised, and respected

Want to know more? The words in bold are explained in the glossary at the back of the book.

Charles Tupper was always up for a challenge. At the age of 12, he sailed across a creek in a hollowed-out log—even though he couldn't swim. As an 18-year-old medical apprentice, he dissected an amputated leg to understand how the bones and muscles worked together. When he was at college, he walked on thin ice to save a drowning man though it was, he said, "waving under my feet like a sheet." And when he thought his daughter was in danger, he travelled thousands of miles by foot, train, stagecoach, and dogsled to bring her home.

Before he went into politics, Charles had been an excellent country doctor, sometimes travelling hundreds of kilometres in a single day to care for his patients. Even after he became a politician, he continued with his love of medicine. In 1866, though he was premier of Nova Scotia, he still worked as the staff surgeon at the Nova Scotia provincial hospital and was the city's **chief medical officer**.

Charles was blunt and always spoke his mind, no matter if it offended anyone.

That's partly why Governor General Lord Aberdeen and his wife didn't like him at all! Lady Aberdeen in particular complained of his rough ways. She thought he was dishonest and always on the lookout for money.

These qualities, however, were just what Prime Minister Macdonald needed in a helper! Macdonald called Charles his "warhorse." Whenever he needed someone to stand up and fight for him, he'd send for Charles.

A man of many careers

When the cholera epidemic of 1866 hit Halifax, Charles put all his energy into fighting the disease and saving lives. Called to the house of a sick little girl, he recognized that she had cholera. He immediately had the house barred up, hitched his own horse to the ambulance, and drove her and her parents to a part of the hospital where people infected with cholera were isolated from the rest of the hospital.

Charles was a man of many careers: doctor, newspaper editor, businessman, politician, and royal commissioner. He was the first physician premier of Nova Scotia and the only physician prime minister of Canada. He served 41 years in politics before becoming prime minister, then lost the position after less than 10 weeks. If two women—a grieving widow (**Agnes Macdonald**) and a member of the British aristocracy (**Lady Aberdeen**)—had had their way, he wouldn't have been named prime minister at all.

From Old Tramp to Boodle Knight

During his life he was hated, knighted, honoured, despised, and respected —often at the same time. What was it about this man that stirred up such strong emotions that he was known as "the Old Tramp" or the "Boodle Knight" to some? (Boodle means the money from a bribe.) Others knew him as the "War Horse of Cumberland County."

Sir Wilfrid Laurier said that Charles was ". . . the most fearless combatant that ever sat in the Parliament of Canada" and "next to [**Sir John A.**] **Macdonald**, the man who did most to bring Canada into **Confederation**." He worked hard to unite the provinces and, as one of the original **Fathers of Confederation**, lived longer than any of the others.

Charles had a strong personality. Some considered him arrogant and a bully. But he was also a man with a tremendous work ethic. He believed in doing things because they were right and beneficial. He was a great mediator, getting opposing sides to work together—a man who wasn't afraid to speak up and to speak out for what he believed in.

Charles's life provides us with a picture of what one person can do if he or she works with commitment, is determined to learn a lot, and uses every ounce of talent to work for a worthwhile goal.

Charles is a man of many careers—doctor, newspaper editor, businessman, politician, and royal commissioner. He serves 41 years in politics before becoming prime minister, then holds the position for less than 10 weeks.

Although Charles is a favourite of Prime Minister Macdonald, he has serious opponents. One of these is Lady Aberdeen, the wife of Canada's governor general. She blocks Tupper's way at every opportunity.

1833

The Tuppers spend a summer in PEI, where 12-year-old Charles and his 10-year-old brother, Nathan, often go out on adventures. On one occasion, Charles and Nathan add a sail to a hollowed-out log and launch across a creek.

All is well until a sudden gust of wind—and "Captain" Charles's quick reaction—plunges them into the water. Unable to swim, they barely make it back to land.

Chapter 1

A hard act to follow

1821
Charles is born.

1823
Charles's brother, Nathan, is born.

1825
Charles's brother, James, is born, but dies soon after.

1828
Charles, age 7, finishes reading the entire Bible to his father.

1829
Charles's sister, Elizabeth, is born.

1836
Charles, now 15, apprentices with Dr. Page.

1837
Charles attends Horton Academy in Wolfville, NS.

1839
Charles apprentices with Dr. Harding.

1840
Charles sails to Scotland to study medicine at the University of Edinburgh.

Charles could settle an argument fast. It was a skill he learned early, as one of 10 children living in a small wooden cabin on a farm near Amherst, Nova Scotia.

Charles's father was also named Charles—Reverend Charles, in fact. Reverend Charles understood 13 languages and had read the Bible in English, Greek, Latin, Hebrew, French, Syriac, German, Italian, Spanish, and Portuguese. He was a Baptist preacher, a school principal, and he wrote for a number of newspapers and magazines.

Reverend Charles's bachelor life changed in a big way when he met Miriam Lockhart Lowe. Miriam was a shy woman, physically delicate and slim of build, who was also devout, intelligent, and knew the Bible inside and out. She was a perfect wife for a minister.

Lots of kids and lots of books

Although Miriam was only 27, she was already a widow with six young children. Her husband had died of consumption. When Reverend Charles married her, his life changed overnight. Instantly he became the father of six children. Over the next 10 years, he and Miriam would add five more to their family: Charlotte, born in 1819; Charles, born on July 2, 1821; Nathan, born in 1823; James, born in 1825 (but he died within a month); and Elizabeth, born in 1829. The house was full of children.

And then there were the books! Whatever space wasn't filled with kids or their belongings was crammed with books. Reverend Charles and Miriam home-schooled their children in the beginning, and by the age of 7, Charles had read the entire Bible to his father. When Charles was 9, his father taught him how to find his direction by using the pole star, in case he ever got lost.

A near-drowning

The Tuppers weren't wealthy but they lived in a home rich with art, music and literature. They believed that studying another language was a way to strengthen the brain. To motivate Charles, his father would pay him a halfpenny for every page that he was able to translate into Latin. Charles was clever and learned quickly. Knowing this made him confident, and maybe even a little arrogant. He believed he could accomplish anything with learning and hard work.

But life was not all schoolwork and church. In 1833, the family moved to Bedeque, Prince Edward Island, for a year. One day when he was 12, Charles and his 10-year-old brother, Nathan, grabbed a hollowed-out log, added a sail, and launched themselves across Wilmot Creek. They might have made it, but a gust of wind—and "Captain" Charles's quick reaction—toppled their makeshift boat and plunged them into the water. Unable to swim, the boys barely made it back to land. They dried out their clothes in the sun, got dressed, and snuck back home. Luckily for them, their parents never found out about their near-drowning, so they didn't get in trouble.

Caring for others

Above all else, the Tuppers instilled in their children two values: a love of learning and a desire to care for others. While the reverend encouraged Charles in his studies, Miriam showed him the importance of selflessness. Charles watched as she nursed many people through the scarletina epidemic. She was like a modern-day public-health nurse, visiting the sick in their homes, and feeding and bathing them until they were well enough to care for themselves.

In those days, epidemics were frequent. Scarlet fever was especially dangerous because it often resulted in death. There were no vaccinations available to protect people, and little in the way of medicine to cure them.

Whoa! Imagine! Charles had ten brothers and sisters. That was lots even for those days!

Plagues and epidemics

Contagious diseases were common in Canada in the 1800s. Fever and ague (later called malaria), cholera, typhoid, smallpox, diphtheria, and typhus all caused a lot of misery, as did tuberculosis, known then as "the consumption." So widespread were these diseases that, in 1860, life expectancy for a male was 40 years. For a female it was slightly higher at 42 years. Compare this to life expectancy for Canadians in 2003: for a male it was 77 years and for a female 82.

Immigration not only brought the people who built the nation to Canada, it also brought disease. In the spring of 1830, all of the Tupper children contracted "scarletina with putrid sore throat." In 1828, construction of the Rideau Canal had to be halted due to malaria. Four years later, cholera killed 600 in Ontario. Carried by travellers, cholera killed over 6,000 Canadians in 1832.

So many settlers died of typhus in 1847 that it became known as the "black year of emigration." Many of these settlers were from Ireland where the **potato famine** of 1846 caused mass starvation and the weakened population was unable to resist the epidemic. When they travelled to Canada seeking a better life, they took typhus with them. Packed tightly into a ship hold, they spread the disease known as ship's fever to the other passengers. There were so many burials at sea that one passenger remarked, "It was nothing but splash, splash, splash all day long."

Some survived the sea voyage, only to die on land. In 1847, 5,424 victims of typhus were buried at Grosse-Île, Quebec. Port towns were especially prone to outbreaks of epidemics. Both crew and passengers could be infected and when they left the ship, they took disease with them.

In 1854, 1,500 people died of cholera in an eight-week period in Saint John, New Brunswick, despite Saint John having established North America's first **quarantine** station in 1785. There, immigrants showing any sign of illness were given a kerosene shower, then a hot water shower. Their clothing and luggage were steam-cleaned.

The dead were often buried in a common grave. In 1966, excavation for an extension to the Kingston General Hospital in Ontario was halted to allow for some of the remains of 1,400 Irish immigrants to be relocated to St. Mary's Cemetery. The immigrants had all died of typhus in the 1847–'48 epidemic.

It was a country doctor in England, Edward Jenner, who showed the world that exposing healthy people to the virus that caused cowpox could protect them from smallpox. This process became known as "vaccination"; since Jenner's time, scientists have found vaccines for many contagious diseases. Smallpox is no longer the great threat it once was, nor are polio, measles, mumps, diphtheria, or rubella. These diseases are now rare in Canada and other developed countries.

Scientists are still looking for a vaccine to prevent the spread of HIV, the "human immunodeficiency virus" that causes AIDS (Acquired Immuno-deficiency Syndrome). Since AIDS was first identified, on December 1, 1981, it has killed more than 25 million people, making it one of the most destructive worldwide epidemics in recorded history.

For more information about plagues and epidemics, visit our website at www.jackfruitpress.com.

Charles studied at Horton Academy in Wolfville, Nova Scotia.

Once, when his teacher gave him some math problems, Charles asked the principal for help.

The principal tried and tried but couldn't solve the problems either. So Charles refused to work on them any longer; he felt that he shouldn't be expected to know any more than the principal himself.

The result? Charles got a bad mark in math.

Perhaps it was Charles's sense of duty and the example of his mother's dedication to nursing the sick that made him decide to become a doctor. At age 15, Charles began an apprenticeship under Dr. Benjamin Page of Amherst, Nova Scotia. After a year of working with Dr. Page, he knew he'd made the right choice. He knew beyond a doubt that he wanted to become a doctor. But first he had to attend the Horton Academy in Wolfville, Nova Scotia, where he studied Latin, Greek, French, and the sciences. He earned some money doing odd jobs and teaching.

Living with Dr. Ebenezer

In November 1839, Charles, now 18, looked for another medical apprenticeship. He wanted to take a four-year degree in medicine at the University of Edinburgh in Scotland, but he knew he could reduce that time by one year if he could get accepted as an apprentice with a more well-known and reputable physician. Shortening his time by a year meant less expense for his family.

So, for 10 months he lived at the home of Dr. Ebenezer Fitch Harding in Windsor, Nova Scotia, where he learned as much as he could about the profession and practice of physician, surgeon, and apothecary (called a pharmacist today). Charles was determined to become the best doctor he could. By day and night, he assisted with the preparation of medicines, delivered babies, and tended to the sick.

One afternoon, Charles watched Harding and another doctor amputate a First Nations patient's leg. Then Dr. Harding gave the leg to Charles so he could dissect it and study the bones and muscles in greater detail. But before Charles could begin, the patient's relatives approached him. They said that, according to their beliefs, unless the leg was buried in sacred ground, the patient would be unable to walk in the afterlife. Charles promised to honour their beliefs. So, when he'd finished studying the amputated limb, he put it in a small box. He waited until dark, then carried the box under his cloak and buried it in the Roman Catholic graveyard.

Six weeks at sea

In order to study at the University of Edinburgh, Charles needed Dr. Harding to write him a strong letter of recommendation. He didn't have to worry because the doctor was pleased with Charles's progress. Harding wrote, "I am highly satisfied with his abilities, correct moral deportment, and with the zeal and diligence he has manifested in the prosecution of the various studies connected with the profession of medicine."

In August 1840, at age 19, Charles set sail from Windsor, Nova Scotia, for Scotland. He'd never been to sea before; his one sailing experience had

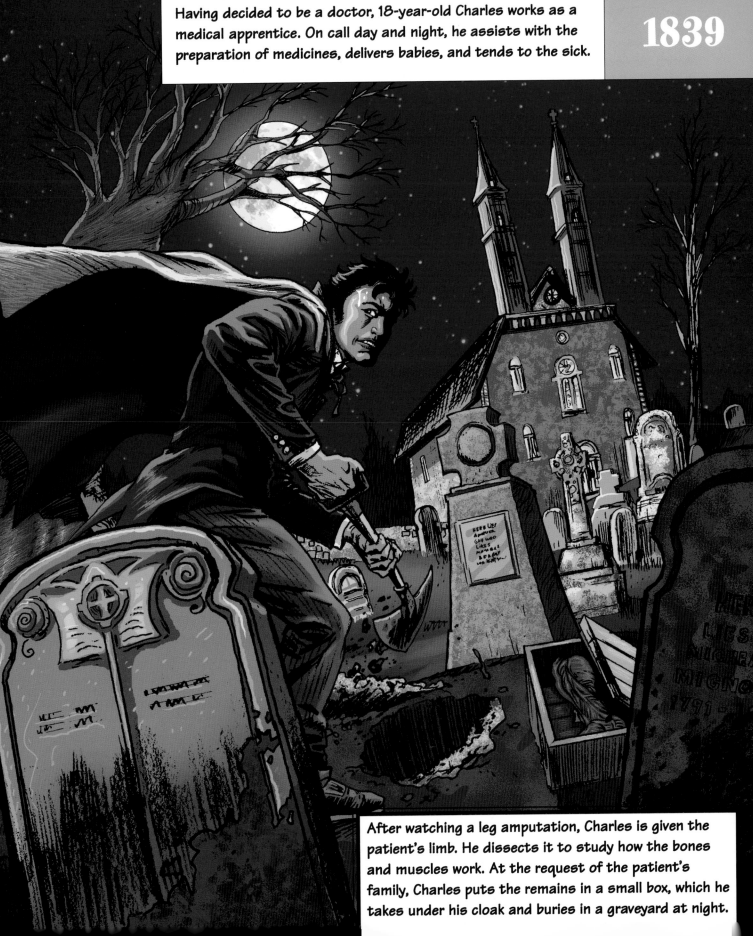

Having decided to be a doctor, 18-year-old Charles works as a medical apprentice. On call day and night, he assists with the preparation of medicines, delivers babies, and tends to the sick.

1839

After watching a leg amputation, Charles is given the patient's limb. He dissects it to study how the bones and muscles work. At the request of the patient's family, Charles puts the remains in a small box, which he takes under his cloak and buries in a graveyard at night.

Charles, out skating one day on a small lake near Edinburgh, saw six people fall through thin ice.

He raced over and tried to pull a drowning man out of the water. Other people saw what was happening and worked to save the other five.

As Charles struggled to save the man, the ice broke beneath him, and he too fell into the freezing water. An iceboat was quickly pulled to the hole and all were pulled out and pushed safely to shore.

Later that evening, as he entered a lecture room, his fellow students stood up and clapped, honouring him for his bravery.

been the hollowed-out log on Wilmot Creek when he and his brother had nearly drowned. He must have been a little hesitant when faced with a six-week sea voyage aboard a ship so loaded with lumber that planks of wood were piled as high as the railings.

A knock-'em-out fight at sea

Charles was one of only two passengers on the brigantine *Huntington*. Also on the ship were the captain, the mate (the second-in-command), and three other crew members. But Charles socialized little; he spent most of the 40-day voyage being seasick.

Maybe that's why the smoke of the mate's pipe made Charles feel ill. He asked him to put it out, but the man refused and Charles punched him, smashing the pipe into a dozen pieces against the man's jaw. The mate sprang at Charles, who fought back with wrestling moves he'd learned at Horton Academy. A crew member who'd been steering the ship left the wheel to separate the two of them. By the time the captain arrived on the scene, the ship was drifting off course. The mate was sent to his bunk for three days and never smoked in Charles's face again.

Docking at Glasgow, Charles regained his land legs and set out by stage-coach to cross Scotland to Edinburgh, where he would attend medical school at the university.

It would be three years before he'd return home to Nova Scotia.

To whom it may concern,

I am highly satisfied with Charles's abilities, correct moral deportment, and with the zeal and diligence he has manifested in the prosecution of the various studies connected with the profession of medicine.

Sincerely,

Dr. Ebenezer Fitch Harding

Now 19, Charles embarks on a six-week voyage to Scotland. Seasick for most of the trip, he socializes little. Coming on deck, he asks the ship's mate to put out his pipe because he's bothered by its smoke.

1840

When the man refuses, Charles punches him in the face. The angry mate jumps at him, but Charles uses the wrestling skills he picked up at Horton Academy. The result? The mate never smokes in Charles's face again.

1843

Eager to apply what he learned at school, 22-year-old Charles invests a great deal of energy in his work. Although his medical practice covers a huge area, he never refuses a sick call, tending to others even when he's sick himself.

Charles does so much travelling to visit patients that he has to stable horses at different barns throughout the county. On one particular day, he travels 160 kilometres by wagon and a further 80 by horseback, caring for three seriously ill patients. When he stops at a house for a cup of tea, he falls so deeply asleep that no one is able to wake him for several hours.

Chapter 2

A tireless doctor

Charles travelled with a cargo of pig iron and bricks, rather than lumber, on his homeward voyage. He had not outgrown his seasickness, and spent much of the 54 sailing days lying on his bunk. Disembarking at Boston, he booked passage on a ship to Saint John, New Brunswick, and from there made his way home to Amherst, Nova Scotia.

It was 1843 and Charles was now a fully trained doctor. While in Edinburgh, Charles had led an active social life that included going to the theatre and drinking alcohol, two behaviours of which his parents heartily disapproved. He had performed well at one of the best medical schools in the world and had travelled throughout England, Scotland, and France.

Charles had learned some of the more advanced practices of the time, like the use of chloroform to ease the pain of childbirth. He also learned that poverty was partly responsible for the spread of diseases, especially during epidemics of cholera and smallpox.

A dedicated doctor who never refused a call

Charles was eager to put all of his education to good use. He was 22 years old, with little money, a lot of knowledge, and a great deal of energy. He invested this knowledge and energy into his medical practice and soon gained a reputation for reliability and dedication.

1843
Charles graduates from the University of Edinburgh.

He opens his medical practice in Amherst, Nova Scotia. He often gets paid with chickens rather than money.

1846
Charles marries Frances Amelia Morse.

1847
Their first child, Emma, is born.

1849
A daughter, Lillie, is born but dies seven months later.

1851
Their son, James, is born.

Charles gets typhus, a disease caused by lice and fleas.

With a family full of lawyers, judges, politicians, and powerful friends, how did Frances ended up marrying a lowly country doctor? Because her father lost the family fortune by lending money to people who never paid him back—so Frances didn't have a big <u>dowry</u>.

Charles wasn't the best of husbands—he couldn't resist the charms of the ladies. Poor Frances had to live with horrible rumours about Charles's relationships with other women! (As a young man, for instance, he coaxed a wealthy woman into paying for part of his education.)

In later years, however, he settled down and enjoyed life with Frances.

Charles began his medical practice in a rural community where farming, logging, and mining were the main occupations. Accidents were common, and working conditions difficult. But despite the lack of trained assistants and sanitary conditions, he lost very few patients. It was said that "if Tupper gave you up, you might as well turn your face to the wall" and die. He never refused a sick call, tending to others even when he was sick himself.

His practice grew until he had patients in communities all across Cumberland County, Nova Scotia. Charles spent so many hours on the road that he had to stable horses at different barns throughout the area. Sometimes a farmer would go into his barn to find his own horse gone, and Charles's there instead. He worked long hours. Stopping once at a patient's house, he asked for a cup of hot tea. Before the tea was ready, he fell so deeply asleep that no one could wake him for several hours. That day he had already travelled 160 kilometres by wagon and a further 80 by horseback—and he still had 30 more to go!

The most eligible bachelors in town

Many of his rural patients paid him in chickens, eggs, and vegetables. One man even paid by shoeing Charles's horse. Eventually, Charles became wealthy—not from being a doctor but from being a clever businessman. He opened a pharmacy to serve his medical practice and was soon driving a fine carriage and pair of horses. In his first year of practice, he made 400 pounds sterling ($14,000 today)—this at a time when a house could be rented for $84 a year.

In 1845, Nathan, his younger brother, would graduate from medical school in Philadelphia, Pennsylvania, then join him in his medical practice and ownership of the pharmacy. The two brothers would prosper and become the most eligible bachelors in town.

Charles's first experience with politics led to a lifelong fascination. It was October 1844 and Charles was watching **Joseph Howe**, a **Liberal**, get into a political debate with **Alexander Stewart**, a **Conservative**. Immediately after the debate, Charles had to leave to care for a patient. The next day, he bumped into Stewart and excitedly told him his impressions of the debate. As Charles was talking, Stewart realized how passionate Charles was about Nova Scotia and sensed that this 23-year-old doctor had a future in politics.

An ideal partner for an aspiring politician

That's probably why Stewart introduced Charles to his niece, **Frances Amelia Morse**. Frances was the ideal partner for an aspiring politician because she came from a wealthy and well-connected family. Her grand-

Impressed with young Charles's prospects for the future, prominent Conservative Alexander Stewart introduces him to his niece, Frances Amelia Morse.

1846

Frances is the ideal partner for an aspiring politician—she comes from a wealthy and well-connected family. Not that this matters much to Charles; he falls in love right away.

Before the 1900s, it was common for families like the Tuppers to lose children under one year old to illness.

High rates of death among babies was an accepted fact of life all over the world.

A big change took place with advances in health care and increased understanding of the causes of childhood illnesses.

parents had founded Amherst. Her uncles included a judge, a Conservative provincial legislative assembly member, and her father was the court chief clerk of the Supreme Court of Nova Scotia.

While some suspected Charles's motives in courting Frances, his future wife was a beautiful and intelligent woman who was fully capable of making her own choice for a husband. Despite having many suitors, she chose Charles and they married on October 8, 1846. Charles was 25, Frances only 20. He and Frances moved into one half of a large, elegant home recently built by her father (her parents lived in the other half). That worked well, for Frances was soon pregnant with their first child and Charles was often away taking care of his patients. In July 1847, Frances gave birth to a daughter, Emma. Two years later, in April 1849, the Tuppers' second child was born, a daughter they named Elizabeth Stewart, or Lillie for short.

Standing by as the flames leaped higher

Only six short weeks later, Frances and the children narrowly escaped death. Charles had headed out to see a patient. Something made him look back, and he saw flames in the distance. Quickly, he turned his horse around and raced back, only to learn that it was his own home that was on fire. Told that his family was safe, he ran to the stable, desperate to rescue a favourite horse. But it was too dangerous and neighbours had to hold him back. Charles could only stand by and watch as the flames leaped higher and hotter, and his home and possessions went up in smoke.

The fire was the beginning of a very difficult period for the Tuppers. On November 30, 1850, baby Lillie died of dysentery (a sickness causing severe diarrhea and vomiting). Charles, a great doctor who had saved countless people, could not save his own infant daughter. In July 1851, his mother died. Then Charles himself fell ill with typhus, a disease carried by lice and fleas. Finally, in October 1851, their luck changed for the better, and Frances gave birth to a son, James Stewart.

Charles gets talked into politics

Local Conservatives were determined to turn Charles into one of their candidates. They felt that his popularity as a country doctor would give him a good chance of beating the current Liberal representative. Charles wanted to serve the party, but feared that it would ruin his medical practice because the campaigning would force him to neglect his patients.

Finally, he agreed to run on the condition that he would quit when the party no longer needed him. The already successful doctor began a new chapter in his life. Charles, the healer of people, was about to take on a bigger project—the government of Nova Scotia.

Only weeks after the birth of the Tuppers' second child, the family narrowly escapes death when a fire breaks out in their house and spreads to their barn. Charles runs to the stable, desperate to rescue a favourite horse.

It's too dangerous. Neighbours have to hold him back. Charles can only stand by and watch as his home and possessions go up in smoke.

1852

Charles knows that he has to speak in front of 3,000 people. He's so nervous that he throws up on his way to the meeting. But when the time comes, he's on stage ready to speak.

When Joseph Howe fails to arrive, Charles is invited to begin without him. When Howe arrives, Charles offers to let him speak, but Howe declines. That was a mistake. Charles fires off a volley of attack against the Liberals and impresses the crowd. Howe is shocked. Charles has completely upstaged him.

Chapter 3

A vision that stretched from coast to coast

In 1851, Joseph Howe, a Liberal, held the seat for Cumberland County, where the Tuppers lived. Amherst itself was a Conservative town. This fact led to a lot of heated political discussions that Charles thoroughly enjoyed. While he treated his patients, they talked politics. When he was home, he talked politics with visitors that included the leader of the Conservative party, **William James Johnston**. It was not at all surprising that a man of Charles's nature, a man of his drive and energy and desire to get things done, would get involved in politics.

1852
Charles makes his first political speech.

1855
His son, Charles Hibbert, is born.

1856
Charles tries to get Britain to support a rail link from Nova Scotia to the Canadas.

1857
Charles is named **provincial secretary** of the Conservative party.

1858
His daughter, Sophy, is born.

The government of Nova Scotia gains control of mining in the colony.

1861
Civil war breaks out in the United States.

1862
His son, William Johnston, is born.

1863
Daughter Sophy, 5, dies.

Charles becomes president of the Medical Society of Nova Scotia.

Charles was very, very serious and rarely smiled. He could talk for hours at a time and never lost an argument. He was forceful and would call people "cowards" or "blockheads" if they didn't see things his way. As you can imagine, some people didn't like him!

Charles and John A. Macdonald's connection began in 1864 when they were working together to create Canada. After Macdonald became prime minister, if he was having trouble getting a job done or if people were giving him a hard time, he'd say, "Call Tupper."

Flutters in his stomach

In March 1852, Charles travelled 33 kilometres to River Philip to meet Thomas Andrew DeWolfe, who would be the new Conservative candidate for the upcoming election. Charles was to bring him back to Amherst for a nomination meeting. Before leaving River Philip, Charles introduced DeWolfe with a short speech, his first on the subject of politics.

His speech so impressed DeWolfe that he asked Charles to introduce him at the upcoming nomination meeting. But the young doctor had never addressed a large crowd before, and discovered he was getting flutters in his stomach just thinking about speaking in front of so many important people. This made him so anxious that he threw up on his way to the meeting. But he didn't let his nervousness get in the way of the job he had to do.

The meeting was to start at 10 o'clock. Charles was there but Joseph Howe had not yet arrived. With 3,000 people standing about, impatiently waiting for the speeches, the sheriff invited Charles onto the stage. Nervousness forgotten, Charles launched into his speech—and then, surprising everybody, went on to say why Howe should not be re-elected.

Wowing the crowd

Howe arrived just then and Charles offered to give way and let him speak. Howe knew that Charles was a physician, not a politician, and wasn't worried about anything that Charles had to say. Charles proceeded to wow the crowd, telling them why they should not vote for Howe. Howe was shocked, but it was too late. Charles had won over the audience.

Howe's Liberals still won that election, but Charles had had a taste of politics, and loved it! The Conservatives encouraged him to run in the next election. However, two concerns needed to be sorted out: his large medical practice and his family. His brother, Nathan, solved the first problem by taking on all of Charles's patients. His family, though, was a cause for worry. Frances was used to him being away on medical calls, but if he were elected, she worried that he'd have to live in the capital, Halifax, for months at a time. Her concerns bothered Charles, who in typical fashion replied, "Do not borrow trouble. I may be defeated."

In the next election, Charles won his seat, beating Howe. When Howe was teased that he'd let a Cumberland boy beat him, he answered, "You will soon discover that I have been defeated by the leader of the Conservative party."

A united front

In his first speech to the Nova Scotia legislature, Charles announced that the Conservatives now supported a rail link to the provinces of **Upper**

Like a few other people of his time, Charles has a vision of Canada as one country. But at this point, the five Canadian colonies are separated by huge distances. Each has its own money, postal system, and tariffs. A railway to the Canadas would change all that.

1856

Lots of people were talking union. Why?

Well, for one thing, Britain wasn't treating the colonies as well as they'd wanted. Britain had made it clear that it was tired of supporting the colonies. It wouldn't even help with the cost of building a railway link.

For another, rights and treaties concerning land or resources were decided in Britain with no input from the colonists.

Finally, uniting the colonies would help protect them from invasion from the United States.

26

Canada and **Lower Canada**. He knew from his travels in Europe that a railroad could unify a country and make trade with other **colonies** and countries possible.

He began the process by meeting with the premiers of New Brunswick and the Canadas (now Ontario and Quebec) to see whether he had their support for a cross-Canada railroad. He also asked for help from the British government, but received none. He then decided that the colonies should present a united front when asking the British government again.

Like a few other forward-thinking people of his time, Charles had a vision of one nation. At this time, there were five colonies separated by huge distances. Each had different money, different postal systems, and tariffs that discouraged trade between them. And each was concerned for its own survival. Charles would have to encourage them to work together.

Although the Conservatives were beaten in the election of 1859, Charles kept his seat. In 1863, he moved his family to Halifax. He and Frances now had five children: Emma, James Stewart, **Charles Hibbert**, Sophy Almon, and William Johnston.

Invasion from the south

The next year, the family was devastated by the loss of a second child. In 1863, their darling five-year-old daughter, Sophy, died of diphtheria. Many families lost at least one child to infectious illnesses, but for Charles the loss was bitter. Once again he'd been unable to save his own child. He took all his grief and channelled it into improving medical services for everyone. He had continued to practise medicine while living in Halifax. When the House was recessed, he increased the number of his patients. When the House was in session, he took on a partner.

But now Charles wanted to make a bigger difference. He introduced a resolution to found a medical school at Dalhousie University. Next, he fought for qualifications for doctors and consistent standards of practice. Then his energy went into fighting for better care of the poor, better conditions in hospitals, and improved medical services. In 1863, he was made president of the **Medical Society of Nova Scotia**. During this time, Charles was still a politician with a vision of one nation. He began working to make the colonies unite as one country, each strengthened by the others. This would protect them from one of his biggest fears—the threat of invasion from the United States.

Medical practice in the 1800s

Early settlers relied on charms and potions to heal their illnesses. Many of these folk remedies were effective, but patients would often try all home remedies they knew of before calling in a physician. By then, the patient was gravely sick and might not respond to even the best medical care. Fear of hospitals prevented some from seeking medical help, with good reason. Little was known of the relationship between germs and the spread of infection, and admission to hospital was often a death sentence.

Home surgeries and amputations were performed on kitchen tables or on boards laid on trestles or kitchen chairs. Anaesthetic was not available, so whiskey or wine was used instead. Because there were no trained nurses, family members, neighbours, and even travelling salesmen would be called upon to pass the surgical instruments or hold the patient down. In 1883, Dr. Abraham Groves performed one of the first appendectomies (surgical removal of the appendix) using only a knife and a needle for instruments, and a horsehair (taken from the doctor's horse's tail) for stitches. One of the first transfusions was done by cutting into a donor's vein and using a rubber piston syringe to draw the blood, then injecting it directly into the patient's arm.

Many physicians, like Charles, trained in Edinburgh, Scotland, although the McGill Faculty of Medicine in Montreal had been founded in 1821. Other schools opened at the University of Toronto and University of Montreal (1843),

Queens University (1854), Dalhousie University (1868), University of Western Ontario (1882), and the University of Manitoba (1883). Students from each of these schools volunteered to serve as stretcher-bearers in the **Northwest Rebellion** of 1885, working alongside the physicians and surgeons of the medical corps. Other trained physicians came to Canada as surgeons with the **Hudson's Bay Company** (HBC) or on exploration trips searching for the Northwest Passage.

The Maritimes had a relatively high number of qualified doctors. In the other areas of British North America, there were not as many qualified doctors. In 1871, of the 1,777 physicians registered with the Ontario Medical Register, only 1,277 were licensed to practise medicine. Few worked at medicine full time, often combining professions such as pharmacist, insurance agent, or mortician to guarantee a more stable income.

Today, doctors make very good incomes, especially because they don't have to rely on their patients for payment—in Canada, doctors are usually paid by the government. In Charles's time, payment for services was often in the form of animal livestock (like chickens or pigs) or produce (like eggs, milk, or vegetables). If there was no money or produce, physicians would submit a petition to the government to be paid for the medical services they'd provided.

For more information about this topic, visit our website at www.jackfruitpress.com.

1864

Charles worries about how a small army of 15,000 British soldiers can defend the colonies against 800,000 trained US troops. He believes that a union of the British colonies is the only way for them to protect themselves against the threat of a US invasion.

1864

Charles becomes premier of Nova Scotia.

The Fathers of Confederation meet in Charlottetown, PEI.

1865

The civil war in the United States ends, with the northern states victorious over the southern states.

1866

Nova Scotia introduces free schooling.

1867

Four colonies become one nation, Canada, under the British North America Act on July 1.

Charles is named Companion of the Bath by Queen Victoria.

Charles helps found and becomes the first president of the **Canadian Medical Association**.

Chapter 4

Fathers of Confederation

The **United States Civil War** started in 1861, when the northern states could not settle their differences with the southern states over trade and slavery. Charles could not help but be concerned. He thought it likely that once the war was over and the United States was reunited, the combined north and south armies would turn their attention to the British colonies. Some politicians in the United States believed in manifest destiny, declaring that their country had the right and destiny to rule all of North America. Charles believed that a union of the British colonies would be the only strong protection against the threat of US invasion. How well could a small army of 15,000 British soldiers defend the colonies against 800,000 trained US troops?

Charles acted quickly and strategically to set up the means to strengthen Canada. When he became premier of Nova Scotia on May 11, 1864, he committed his party to an expanded railway network. The train wouldn't just connect the Maritime provinces; it would connect all the colonies and territories of Canada. And it would be

Nova Scotia's schools were in a sorry state when Charles was premier. Parents had to pay to send their kids to school, so lots of kids couldn't go. But even if they could, there was no way of telling how good their education would be.

Charles introduced the Free School Act to improve schools and provide education for all of Nova Scotia's kids.

This new school system would be run by the government and paid for with tax money. Charles knew it was risky—he might lose the next election for raising people's taxes—but that didn't stop him from doing what he felt was right.

more than a link—its path would determine where towns would grow. Charles was drawing up the map for a united Canada!

Why can't we be friends?

At the same time as he was preparing the way for a national railroad, Charles was also pushing for a union of the Maritime colonies. These were Nova Scotia, New Brunswick, and Prince Edward Island (PEI). These colonies had much in common; most of the people depended on farming, fishing, mining, ship building, and forest products to make a living. Rather than trading with each other, though, they traded with Britain. They tended not to cooperate.

Charles pushed ahead, arranging a meeting for September 1, 1864, in Charlottetown, PEI, to discuss Maritime union. He invited seven representatives of the two parties from Canada East and West (as Ontario and Quebec were then called). The **governor general** from Upper and Lower Canada had sent a letter to Charles proposing that a group from the government come to talk about a union of all the colonies. They were so eager to get started, they boarded a steamer and travelled down the St. Lawrence as quickly as possible to join the Charlottetown group.

A botheration scheme

Everyone at the Charlottetown conference, 36 men in all, were later named the Fathers of Confederation. They met again in Quebec on October 10, and firmed up the blueprint for Confederation of the colonies. They worked out a system for one big country. The plan was complicated. There would be a prime minister, not a president, and it would be based on the British system, not the American. At both conferences, one of the really active players was Charles. He happily put forth ideas to these pro-Confederation people, arguing strenuously for union and pledging Nova Scotia's part, but he had yet to go back and convince Nova Scotians to agree to his idea of Confederation.

And in Nova Scotia there was resistance. Charles had a majority government and felt that the resolutions agreed upon in Quebec about the future **Canadian Constitution** would be passed by the Nova Scotia legislature without a problem. However, when the Quebec Resolutions were made public, many people opposed them. The most vocal was former premier Joseph Howe, who wrote a series of anonymous letters to the Halifax newspaper the *Morning Chronicle*, in which he called the plan to unite the colonies a "Botheration Scheme." But then Charles got a boost

What's in a name?
How Canadians almost became Cabotians

Have you ever wondered why you're a Canadian and not a Mesopelagian? Ever questioned why you fly Air Canada instead of Air Transylvania, or why you've been spared the misfortune of watching *Efisgian Idol* on TV?

Well, the truth is, if it weren't for a bunch of mistakes, misinterpretations, and chance encounters, you might very well have been called something other than "Canadian."

True, people started calling our country Canada shortly after **Jacques Cartier** discovered the St. Lawrence River (or the *grande rivière de Hochelaga*, as it was known then). But it wasn't until the Constitutional Act of 1791 that Canada (as in "Upper" and "Lower") was officially recognized as a name. Not that this secured its future; many years later, with Confederation in the offing, over 30 other names were proposed for our fledgling country, such as:

> Acadia, Albertland, Albertoria, Albionora, Albona, Alexandrina, Aquilonia, Borealia, Britannica, Cabotia, Canadensia, Colonia, Efisga (made by taking the first letter of England, France, Ireland, Scotland, Germany, and aboriginal), Hochelaga, Laurentia, Mesopelagia, Niagarentia, New Albion, Norland, Superior, Transatlantica, Transylvania, Tuponia (made from The United Provinces of North America), Ursalia, Vesperia, Victorialand, and Victorialia.

If these names strike you as stupid, well, they struck people as stupid then too. In an 1865 debate, **D'Arcy McGee**, the journalist, politician, and Father of Confederation said, "Now I ask any honourable member of this House how he would feel if he woke up some fine morning and found himself instead of a Canadian, a Tuponian or a Hochelagander."

So where exactly did the name Canada come from? A lot of theories have floated around over the years—most of them pretty unlikely. As Alan Rayburn tells us in his book *Naming Canada*, some people thought it came from Spanish explorers who scouted the land for gold but came up empty handed. "*Aca nada!*" they said. ("Here nothing!")

Another hypothesis revolved around a French guy named Cane (Cane-ada . . . get it?) who tried and failed to establish a settlement here. Yet another was that early French settlers demanded a "can a day" of beer from the bosses of their colony.

The most likely theory, however, is that "Canada" comes from the Huron word *kanata*, meaning village. *Kanata* originally referred to an Iroquoian territory near what is now Quebec City. Jacques Cartier heard the term, wrote it down in his journals, and brought it back to France. Pretty soon everyone there was using it—incorrectly—to describe the whole of New France.

So, if you're happy to be a Canadian and you're looking for someone to thank, start with Cartier. If it weren't for him, you could be singing the Niagarentian national anthem right now.

ALDERSHOT HIGH SCHOOL LIBRARY
50 FAIRWOOD PLACE. W.
BURLINGTON, ONTARIO
L7T IF5   637-2383

For more information about this topic, visit our website at www.jackfruitpress.com.

from an unlikely ally: the **Fenians**. On April 10, 1866, Charles made a motion for Confederation in the Nova Scotia legislature.

Unlikely allies

The Fenians were radical Irish-Americans who opposed Britain's rule in Ireland. They had fled to the United States, but delighted in causing havoc for Britain in North America. Rumours were flying that three ships of Fenians had left New York and were on the way to invade the **Maritimes**. Telegraph message after telegraph message reported that they were getting closer. Charles used this Fenian threat to strengthen his argument for the colonies standing together in protection of their land. When citizens of Halifax witnessed British troops boarding the warship *Duncan* on their way to do battle with the Fenians, he won his motion in the legislature for Confederation with a vote of 31 to 19.

The Fenians were quickly defeated as they tried to invade Campobello Island. Some people noticed that once the resolution to unite was passed, the Fenian problem vanished in the Maritimes. In the fall of 1866, Charles and the rest of the delegates from Canada East and West, Nova Scotia, and New Brunswick headed to London, settling in at the Westminster Palace Hotel to finish the work of achieving their dream of Confederation. For 20 days, the delegates discussed what they wanted the final bill to create Canada to look like. Then, on Christmas Day, Prime Minister Macdonald announced to the British secretary of state that the blueprint for Canada was ready.

A blueprint for Canada

The amazing thing was that the final document looked almost exactly the same as the document they had drawn up at the Quebec conference two years earlier. On July 1, 1867, the **British North America (BNA) Act** came into effect, creating a country of 3.5 million people. Canada East became Quebec and Canada West became Ontario, joining with Nova Scotia and New Brunswick to make the Dominion of Canada. Prince Edward Island and Newfoundland decided not to join, choosing instead to remain colonies. But Charles was content. He'd won his prize.

Ever heard of New Ireland? That's what the Fenians planned to call Canada when they captured it. They were going to hold the country hostage until Great Britain gave Ireland its independence.

The Fathers of Confederation. Charles is fourth from the left.

Hoping to force Britian into pulling its troops out of Ireland, Fenians plot a surprise invasion of Canada. A ragtag force of some 1,000 soldiers sets sail for Campobello Island, near the US border in New Brunswick.

1866

Soon realizing that they have no hope of succeeding against the Canadian militia, British warships, and US authorities, the Fenian commanders withdraw.

1869

Charles's daughter Emma and her husband are in Red River in the middle of the Métis uprising. Although it's December and there's no railway to get there, Charles heads out to retrieve her. He travels thousands of kilometres by train, stagecoach, horse, dogsled, and foot.

Chapter 5

Charles rides into the West

1867
Charles wins a seat in the House of Commons in Ottawa.

The first meeting of the Canadian Parliament takes place on November 6.

1868-1870
Charles continues to practise as a doctor in Ottawa.

1869
Charles "rescues" Emma from the Red River Rebellion.

1870
Charles helps Macdonald write the National Policy.

Manitoba joins the Dominion of Canada.

After Confederation, Charles ran for the new federal Parliament in the 1867 election, and became the only pro-Confederation Nova Scotian member to be elected. He still represented Cumberland County, but now did so in the **House of Commons**, in Ottawa. But Charles was above all a family man. He often took Frances or one of the children with him on business trips, and each time he moved, he moved his family with him: first to Halifax, then to Ottawa. When away from home, he wrote long and frequent letters to them. So you can imagine his distress when, in the fall of 1869, he learned about the **Métis** uprising (**Red River Rebellion**)—and that his daughter, Emma, and her husband, Captain D. R. Cameron, were in the middle of it!

The newly married Emma had accompanied her husband on his assignment as captain of a small troop of soldiers on escort duty for **William McDougall**. McDougall had been sent to head the new government of the Northwest Territories, which the Hudson's Bay Company would transfer to Canada on December 1, 1869.

But the Métis wanted to be consulted about the transfer of the land. They worried that such a change would take away their traditional lands and rights to their own way of life.

In 1885, Louis Riel led a second protest against the Canadian government—the Northwest Rebellion.

First Nations peoples and Métis wanted the government to keep its promise of giving them the food, money, medicine, tools, and training they needed to make the switch from buffalo hunting to farming.

Native chiefs <u>Big Bear</u> and <u>Poundmaker</u> wanted a peaceful settlement to this problem but they couldn't control the angry men in their bands.

After the fighting ended, Big Bear and Poundmaker surrendered and were sentenced to three years in jail. Louis Riel was sentenced to death and hanged.

Charles to the rescue!

Frances begged Charles to get their only surviving daughter. Although it was late fall and winter travel in the west could be dangerous, Charles immediately left Nova Scotia for Ottawa. While there, Sir John A. asked Charles to find out what was going on with the Métis uprising. Charles then travelled from Ottawa to Toronto. On December 13, 1869, he left Toronto by train heading to St. Cloud, Minnesota—as far west as one could get by train. From there, he found a guide and together they boarded a stagecoach to Fort Abercrombie in Dakota. The snow was deep and it was already very cold. While at the fort, they used a dogsled to reach the isolated Hudson's Bay post at Georgetown in -30°C weather. There they met with McDougall—who hadn't been out of his clothes for two months because he was in constant fear for his life—and camped out on buffalo hides in the deep snow.

In the morning, they retraced the route back to Fort Abercrombie. Once there, they got on a horse-drawn sled to make their way along the Red River toward Pembina, where Emma was staying.

Finally, after travelling thousands of miles by train, stagecoach, horse, dogsled, and foot, he located Emma—safe in Pembina. When Emma saw her father walk into the log cabin where she and her husband were staying, she looked up at him and said, "What did you come for?"

Trains, trade, and tariffs

Charles thoroughly enjoyed his western adventure. His difficulty getting west to Emma convinced him to keep pressing for a speedy completion of the **Canadian Pacific Railway**. He was Prime Minister Macdonald's greatest helper.

In 1879, Charles and Macdonald introduced a plan called the National Policy. This policy, they hoped, would create a solid Canadian economy that would support Confederation. They wanted it to achieve three things. The first was to protect Canadian manufacturers from unfair trade with the United States. The second, to ensure that a transcontinental railway was built. The third, to encourage immigration to the West and to provide a home market for buying and selling goods. This policy and the railway did much for Canada's great expansion westward, and discouraged the United States from claiming parts of the West, which later joined Canada.

What was Louis Riel fighting for?

If a bunch of government representatives were to arrive on your street, announce that they now owned the land you lived on, and started making plans to change the shape and size of your property, how would you feel?

This is what happened to the Métis and other people living in the Red River Colony (an area that's now the southern part of Manitoba and northern North Dakota and Minnesota). For most of 200 years, the Hudson's Bay Company (HBC) managed and controlled all the land, including the Red River Colony, that was drained by rivers that flowed into Hudson Bay. This vast piece of the North American continent was named Rupert's Land.

In the 1800s, residents of the Red River Colony were mainly French-speaking Métis and other English-speaking people of First Nations and European descent. Although there were conflicts over language, religion, and class, the colony was evolving into a successful multiracial society. However, the US, British, and Canadian governments were fed up with the HBC's control over such a big part of the continent. When the HBC finally agreed to give up control of Rupert's Land, many American and Canadian newcomers poured into the Red River Colony and began to threaten the locals' land rights and culture.

During negotiations over who would get control of the area, no one invited long-term residents to take part. They were invisible. Prime Minister Sir John A. Macdonald admitted as much when he wrote this to **George-Etienne Cartier**, a member of his government: "All these poor people know is that Canada has bought the country from Hudson's Bay Company and that they are handed over like a flock of sheep to us." On March 20, 1869, the HBC sold Rupert's Land to Canada.

Before the actual transfer took place, Sir John A. sent a team of surveyors to start laying out the boundaries of the future townships. But the land was already divided up by the people who lived there. Like in Quebec, plots started at the river and went back in long, thin strips. Sir John, however, wanted to impose his control by changing it to a different grid system, much like in Ontario.

On October 11, **Louis Riel** stood on a chain that surveyors were using to survey his cousin's farm and demanded that they stop. This was the first act of the Red River Rebellion and in doing this, Riel won the reputation of having stared down the Canadian government. He organized a provisional government that invited all the people of the Red River area, both French- and English-speaking, to discuss the transfer to Canada. After these consultations, he issued the "Declaration of the People of Rupert's Land and the Northwest" and a "List of Rights." He held meetings with representatives from Canada and the HBC. When Canadian prisoners were taken and then released by Riel's men, things didn't go smoothly. One Canadian prisoner was executed, a tragedy that made Riel a wanted man in Ontario and a hero in Quebec.

Negotiations ended with the creation of the Manitoba Act, passed in May 1870. When the transfer took place in July, the Métis were granted land for their own use and bilingual services in the new province.

The result may be thought of as a victory for the Métis. But how could this whole transfer of land been done to avoid so much violence?

For more information about this topic, visit our website at www.jackfruitpress.com.

1884

As high commissioner, Charles watches and defends Canada's interests in England. So when British inspectors reject three shiploads of Canadian cattle, saying they're diseased, Charles rushes to the scene and proves that none of the cattle is infected.

Chapter 6

The reign of the warhorse

Charles knew that, for years, ships from Boston and other US ports on the eastern seaboard had been fishing off the coast of Canada. This cut into the profits of Canadian fishermen. Knowing how dependent the Maritime economy was on its fisheries, Charles pushed for a settlement to this problem.

He influenced Sir John A. Macdonald—who was sent to Washington as part of a British team to negotiate a solution—to seek a fair payment. The resulting **Washington Treaty** led to a payment of $5.5 million to Canada in exchange for 12 years of American fishing off the Canadian coast.

In 1883, while still serving as minister of railways and canals, Charles was appointed **high commissioner** to the United Kingdom. He and Frances moved to London. In his new job, he promoted and defended Canada's interests abroad like a cheerleader for Canada and all things Canadian. Whenever Sir John A. Macdonald needed his "warhorse," however, Charles would return to Canada and get things done.

Double trouble

Charles's two jobs caused him trouble. Holding a cabinet post plus the job of high commissioner meant that he was collecting two salaries. This wasn't allowed by Parliament. So Charles resigned his cabinet post. He rather enjoyed mixing with the aristocracy in London and intended to take the position of high commissioner seriously. He was there to "watch, defend, and guide the interests of the Dominion." It was a position ideally suited for someone of his skills.

When Charles learned that inspectors at the port of Liverpool had rejected three shiploads of Canadian cattle saying they were infected with **anthrax**, he knew the inspectors would condemn the cattle and

---

1871
The Washington Treaty resolves the Canada–United States fishing dispute.

1879
Charles is knighted by Queen Victoria.

1881
Charles's father dies.

1883-87
Charles is appointed high commissioner to Great Britain.

1886
Charles is decorated with the Knight Grand Cross of St. Michael and St. George by Queen Victoria.

1888
Charles is created Baron Tupper by Queen Victoria.

1896
Charles becomes prime minister, but only for 68 days.

1900
Charles loses his seat in the election.

1901
Charles and Frances move to England.

1912
Frances dies after 66 years of marriage.

1915
Charles dies and his body is carried home in the warship *Metagama* (shown below). After a state funeral, he's buried beside Frances in Halifax.

So what exactly did Charles do during his 68 days as PM?

Well, around that time, the rights of French-speaking Catholics in Manitoba's school system was a hot issue. Charles pushed for a bill that would secure their rights to an education.

Charles was worried that conflicts over religion or language would weaken our fledgling country.

After six weeks of debate in the House of Commons, the bill was blocked. Charles was forced to call an election—and he lost to Wilfrid Laurier's Liberal party.

stop future shipments from Canada. He couldn't let that happen because Canada depended on this market to sell its beef. After dissecting a sampling of the animals, he was able to prove beyond a doubt that not one was diseased.

He not only saved the beef industry during his time in London, he also pushed for improvements in services for Canada. In 1886, he got financial help from Britain for a steamship service from Vancouver to China and Japan. In 1887, he ensured that iron and steel were added to the goods protected by tariffs.

But time was passing. Charles had adult grandchildren and his friends were dying off. He had no interest in returning to Parliament, though. He had a job that earned him lots of respect. He loved living in London and travelling around Europe, and saw how hard the PM's job was on his old friend Sir John A., who died in 1891.

After Macdonad's death, the party wanted **John Thompson** to lead, but he stepped aside for John Abbott, who led Parliament from the **Senate**. In failing health, Abbott handed over the position to Thompson after 17 months. Thompson died in office two years later.

Charles wins his prize . . .

Charles was the logical choice to become prime minister when Thompson died in 1894. But it was the governor general's duty to name the next PM and Governor General **Lord Aberdeen** and his wife didn't like Charles. They passed him over to appoint **Mackenzie Bowell**.

Finally, though, Lord Aberdeen had no choice but to appoint Charles, when seven members of Bowell's cabinet resigned because of his inability to handle the **Manitoba Schools Question**. Manitoba wanted no Catholic schools, but the British government demanded that the Canadian government deal with it themselves by reinstating the Catholic schools. Bowell resigned and, on May 1, 1896, at 74 years of age, Charles became the sixth prime minister of the Dominion of Canada. But it was to be a bittersweet victory for Charles. He had to call an election because the current government had already been in power for five years. He had only two short months to show Canada that the Conservative party could lead without Macdonald. But the people wanted a change, and the elegant and popular Liberal leader, Wilfrid Laurier, offered them just that.

. . . But loses it soon after

Campaigning to the end, Charles and his party went down to defeat in the election of June 1896. He tried to stay in power by appealing to several ridings where the votes had been close. He even tried to convince Lord Aberdeen to let him stay on. When he finally resigned, he had been prime minister for only 68 days. He became leader of the Opposition and

Bullying, aggression, and assertiveness

Was Sir Charles Tupper really a bully? People who faced off with him would probably have said yes. Others might disagree and explain instead that Charles was only being aggressive or assertive.

People who are bullies try to control others. They want to be in charge and prefer to hurt people to get what they want. In a debate, Charles would badger and dominate his opponent, trying to get them to see things his way. This may have left them feeling bullied. During this time, many people got away with bullying because being "forceful" was seen as a sign of leadership, strength, and manliness.

This is no longer true. Bullying is now seen as unacceptable whether it is at home, at school, at work or in the community. Bullies aim to embarrass their targets and make them feel unwanted and unpopular. They are easy to spot because they mistreat others by injuring them or hurting their feelings. They sometimes use physical force or threats. Other times, they use cruel nicknames or spread gossip. Some bullies are sneaky with their actions, blaming people for things they did not do. No matter how you slice it, a bully's specialty is to make his (or her) victims feel worthless.

Aggressive people may criticize others and try to intimidate them, but do not usually try to control them or make them feel bad. They want to persuade people to agree with their ideas and way of thinking. Aggressive people often speak in a loud voice, no matter how many people can hear what they say. Everyone knows what an aggressive person thinks, because he (or she) makes sure to tell everybody and to loudly challenge anyone who feels differently.

Assertive people can present their ideas without needing to persuade others to their way of thinking. They can have strong opinions and beliefs but respect that everyone has a right to their own beliefs and opinion. Assertive people may offer advice, but accept that it is a person's choice to accept that advice or reject it. They may try to influence people's opinion but never try to over-rule them.

Charles's commitment to whatever task he was assigned might have made some people feel uncomfortable, but it also convinced people to vote for him and his Conservative party. For instance, during the election campaign of 1891, when Charles was almost 70 years old, he travelled 6,000 km over 34 days, giving countless speeches that no doubt helped Macdonald win the election.

Consider how you defend your ideas. The important thing is that everyone gets a chance to express themselves and that we learn to behave in ways that support and nuture everyone around us. As the students of Mono-Amaranth Public School in Ontario are discovering, bullying can be stopped if we learn to RESPECT each other.

RESPONSIBILITY
EFFORT
SAFETY
PARTICIPATION
EXCELLENCE
COURTESY
TRUST

Bullying can be stopped if we learn to "RESPECT" each other.

For more information about this topic, visit our website at www.jackfruitpress.com.

Charles was mixed up in several scandals over the years, each of which was reported in the press. At various times he was accused of:

- holding two jobs and receiving a salary for each (conflict of interest)

- giving jobs to friends (patronage)

- hiring family members (nepotism)

- making money from railway shares (fraud)

- inappropriate relationships with women

worked hard to rebuild the fortunes of the Conservative party. And though he campaigned with his usual amazing strength in the election of 1900, Laurier's Liberals won again and Charles even lost his own seat. Charles was shattered—it was his first riding defeat in his entire political career of 13 elections. He recognized that it was time to let someone else lead the Conservative party. Charles Hibbert (Charles's son, who was a **member of Parliament**) nominated **Robert Borden**, who brought the Conservatives back to power in 1911.

Life after politics

Charles and Frances moved back to England in 1901, where they lived with their daughter, Emma, and her family in her grand old home in Bexleyheath, Kent, near London. Yet even in retirement he had work to do! Charles learned to speak and write Italian. He also kept busy writing his memoirs and letters to newspapers and politicans about topics that were important to him.

Charles was distraught when Frances died in May 1912 at the age of 86. They'd been married for 66 years. Charles took her body home to Nova Scotia to bury her. Then he went west to Vancouver to visit his son.

At the end of his visit, he said goodbye to Canada in his own way. He boarded a train in Vancouver and crossed the country that he'd played so great a part in building. Each mile and stopover must have had memories for him—of battles fought and adventures lived. He arrived finally in Amherst, Nova Scotia, where his story had begun, to find that the town had put on a party for him, the kind of party that had never been seen before or since. Prime Minister Borden and thousands of people joined him for a week-long celebration.

The warhorse returns

On May 1, 1913, Charles returned to England. Even though he lived with his daughter Emma, he missed his darling Frances terribly. He dreamed of her many times and recorded these dreams in his journal. He also mourned the death of his son, James Stewart, who'd died in April 1915, and worried about his grandson, Reggie, who'd been wounded on the battlefields of France during **World War I**.

When Charles died on October 30, 1915, at the age of 94, his friend, Sir John A. Macdonald, had been dead for a quarter of a century. Newspapers praised his achievements and gave him the public approval so often denied him in life. It was fitting that this last Father of Confederation was transported home to Canada on the warship *Metagama*, for Charles had been a warrior all his life. Following his state funeral, a procession of 5,000 troops from Nova Scotia and overseas battalions followed his casket to St. John's Cemetery in Halifax. He was buried beside his beloved Frances while a 17-gun salute rang out. The warhorse had come home.

Charles and Frances move to England, where they live with their daughter, Emma, and her family in her grand old home in Bexleyheath, Kent. At this time, another honour from Queen Victoria makes him Baron Tupper. Yet he still has work to do!

1901

NAPOLI

ENGLISH-
ITALIAN
DICTIONARY

Charles learns to speak and write Italian. He also writes letters to newspapers and politicians and works on his memoirs. When his 86-year-old wife, Frances, dies in 1912, Charles travels back to Canada to bury her in Halifax. He also visits his son in British Columbia. Once back in England, Charles misses his "darling Frances" terribly. He dreams of her many nights and records these dreams in his journal.

Sir Charles Tupper:

"The human mind naturally adapts itself to the position it occupies. The most gigantic intellect may be dwarfed by being cabin'd, cribbed, and confined. It requires a great country and great circumstances to develop great men."

Sir Charles Tupper
1865

Charles believed in hard work. He set goals for himself and his country, and he worked hard to achieve them. Throughout his life he acted with integrity—once he'd given his word, he kept his promise even if it meant certain defeat at the polls. He was a man of vision, a man who recognized early on what Canada could become.

He based his political career on the belief that Canadians should play down their cultural and ethnic differences and instead focus their energies on developing the vast resources of this country. He also believed that every child, regardless of sex, colour, or religion, had the right to an education.

When Charles entered politics, the British colonies had five different tariffs, currencies, and postal systems. He eventually combined them into one. He brought back to Nova Scotia the royalties from its mines, which had been, by tradition, paid to England's Duke of York.

He defended the livelihoods of Maritime fishermen through a treaty with the United States and Great Britain. He protected Canada's coal, iron, and steel industries by demanding higher tariffs. He refused to allow Britain to reject Canadian fish and cattle. In his hands, the office of Canadian high commissioner to Britain gained respect.

Charles, together with Sir John A. Macdonald, worked to bring about Confederation, then struggled to ensure that

A relentless commitment

the National Policy brought economic benefits to each province. Charles fought for the completion of the transcontinental railroad (Canadian Pacific Railway) to link the country together and to carry immigrants and trade goods to the West. He never doubted that he'd succeed in building this railroad—a task that was considered the "greatest venture ever attempted by a nation of five million (people)."

In 1865, he set up a system of free primary education in Nova Scotia, yet still upheld the rights of Roman Catholics for a separate school. Then he reorganized Nova Scotia's education system so that it was governed by a council free of religious ties. This brought about "religious harmony unparalleled in the colonies."

Charles kept his interest in medicine when he entered politics. He insisted on improved health care for rich and poor alike, lobbied for better hospitals, and brought about better, standardized training for doctors. He supported provincial and national medical associations, and a medical training school for Nova Scotia.

Charles had his faults. In debate, he could dominate to the point of bullying. He made up rules as he went along, cutting corners to get what he thought best for the country. He could be ruthless, earning enemies, but he promoted talented people in the civil service and the Conservative party, a move that won him respect among both politicians and government employees.

Sir Charles was probably the most experienced and capable statesman that Canada ever had. Many of the programs he fought for are still in existence. One can only wonder what he might have accomplished if he'd had more time as prime minister.

Timeline: The life and times of Sir Charles Tupper

YEAR	CHARLES'S LIFE	EVENTS IN CANADA AND THE WORLD
1821	Charles is born on July 2 near Amherst, Nova Scotia.	The Montreal General Hospital is incorporated. Napoleon Bonaparte, emperor of France (1799–1815), dies in exile on the island of St. Helena.
1823	Brother Nathan is born.	
1829	Sister Charlotte is born.	Slavery is abolished in Mexico.
1836	Charles finishes school and apprentices as a doctor with Dr. Benjamin Page in Amherst.	
1837	Charles returns to school at Horton Academy in Wolfville, Nova Scotia.	Victoria becomes Queen of England.
1839	Charles apprentices from November to August 1840 with Dr. Ebenezer Harding in Windsor, Nova Scotia.	Lumbermen from New Brunswick and Maine clash over the undefined border in what becomes known as the Aroostook War.
1840	Charles sails to Scotland to study medicine at the University of Edinburgh.	
1841		The Queen sanctions the union of Upper and Lower Canada on July 23 under a central government. Upper Canada's name is changed to Canada West. Lower Canada's name is changed to Canada East.
1842		The Northeastern Boundary Dispute between New Brunswick and Maine is settled by Webster-Ashburton Treaty. Construction of the first railway in Nova Scotia begins.
1843	Charles graduates as a doctor. He returns to Amherst to begin practising medicine.	Fort Victoria is built by Britain to strengthen its claim to Vancouver Island. The Cornwall and Chambly canals are officially opened.
1844		Construction of the first railway in New Brunswick begins.
1846	Charles marries Frances Amelia Morse.	British prime minister Robert Peel announces free trade. This ends the old colonial trade system.
1847	Daughter Emma is born.	The St. Lawrence Canal is completed.
1849	Daughter Lillie is born and dies at age 7 months.	
1850		The Fugitive Slave Act is passed in the USA. This results in free and enslaved black peoples fleeing to British North America.
1851	Charles's mother, Miriam, dies. Son James is born.	The first Canadian postage stamp is issued.
1854		Reciprocity begins between British North America and the USA. The Crimean War takes place in the Balkans and the Crimean Peninsula (1854–1856): Russia fights the Ottoman (Turkish) Empire and its allies (Britain, France, and Sardinia).
1855	Charles defeats Joseph Howe in an election for a seat in the Legislative Assembly of Nova Scotia. Son Charles Hibbert is born.	Bytown is renamed Ottawa. The first train crosses Niagara Falls on a suspension bridge.

More on the life and times of Sir Charles Tupper

YEAR	CHARLES'S LIFE	EVENTS IN CANADA AND THE WORLD
1857	Charles becomes provincial secretary in the newly formed Conservative government.	Ottawa becomes the capital of the Province of Canada. The revolt of 1857 occurs when India fights for freedom from British rule.
1858	Daughter Sophy is born. Charles tries to get support for an intercolonial railway from the government.	The Fenian Brotherhood, the US wing of the Irish Republican Brotherhood (IRB), a secret revolutionary group, is founded in Dublin. It's composed of immigrants and Irish Americans who want to free Ireland from British rule.
1859	Charles keeps his seat but the Conservatives are defeated in Nova Scotia.	Abraham Shadd becomes the first black person elected to public office in Canada.
1860	Charles moves to Halifax and begins a medical practice. He is appointed city medical officer. He is a political editor at the *British Colonist* newspaper.	Construction begins on the House of Commons. Several Fenian raids take place.
1861		The US Civil War (1861–1865) begins: President Abraham Lincoln and the northern states want to abolish slavery. The southern states form a provisional Confederate government and go to war against the North. The North wins and slavery is ended.
1862	Youngest son William is born.	
1863	Charles wins his seat and the Conservatives are returned to power in Nova Scotia. His daughter Sophy dies of diphtheria.	London's Metropolitan, the world's first underground passenger railway, opens to the public.
1864	Charles becomes premier of Nova Scotia. He organizes a meeting in Charlottetown, PEI, to discuss union of the Maritimes and then the rest of the British North American colonies. Another conference is held in Quebec.	The international Red Cross is founded in Geneva, Switzerland.
1865	Charles introduces and wins support for the Act of Education, which provides residents of Nova Scotia free, non-religious schools.	Slavery is abolished in the United States. The Salvation Army is founded in London, England, to serve the poor and homeless.
1866	Charles introduces legislation in the Nova Scotia legislature to allow Confederation with other provinces. It passes.	Several Fenian raids take place on the border with the United States.
1867	Charles is awarded the Companion of the Bath.	Canadian Confederation takes effect on July 1. John A. Macdonald becomes the first prime minister of Canada (1867–1873).
1868	Charles travels to London to defend Confederation against those who oppose it. He sets up his medical practice in Ottawa.	The Federal Militia Act creates the first Canadian army.

Still more on the life and times of Sir Charles Tupper

YEAR	CHARLES'S LIFE	EVENTS IN CANADA AND THE WORLD
1869	Charles's daughter Emma marries Captain D. R. Cameron of the Royal Artillery, who is posted to Fort Garry (now Winnipeg, Manitoba). Charles travels from Halifax to where his daughter is staying to bring her and her husband back to Nova Scotia.	Métis leader Louis Riel seizes Fort Garry, Winnipeg, during the Red River Rebellion. He protests the Canadian government not consulting with the Métis people before the Hudson's Bay Company handed over its land to the Canadian government.
1870	Charles is named president of the Privy Council.	Thomas Scott is executed under Louis Riel's provisional government. Northwest Territories and the province of Manitoba are created.
1871		British Columbia joins Confederation.
1872	Charles becomes the minister of inland revenue.	The first nationwide labour protest is held. Asian and aboriginal peoples are banned from voting in BC.
1873	Charles is appointed minister of customs.	Sir John A. Macdonald is forced to resign as prime minister because of the Pacific Scandal. Prince Edward Island joins the Dominion of Canada. Alexander Mackenzie becomes the second prime minister of Canada (1873–1878). The North West Mounted Police force is formed.
1875		The Supreme Court of Canada is established. The Indian Act is passed.
1878	Charles becomes minister of public works.	Sir John A. Macdonald is elected for a second term as prime minister (1878–1891). The Canada Temperance Act is passed.
1879	Charles is appointed minister of railways and canals. He proposes the creation of the Canadian Pacific Railway. He is knighted by Queen Victoria.	The Anglo-Zulu War takes place in South Africa: Britain wins and takes over control of Zululand. The War of the Pacific (1879–1883) begins: Peru, Bolivia, and Chile fight over borders and natural resource.
1881	Charles's father, Rev. Charles Tupper, dies.	
1883	Charles is appointed high commissioner to Great Britain.	The Sino-French War (1883–1885) starts: France and China fight over Vietnam. In the end, Vietnam is divided. China controls the north, France gets the south.
1884	Charles resigns from cabinet as minister of railways and canals.	
1885		The Canadian Pacific Railway is completed. The Northwest Rebellion takes place. Louis Riel is hanged for treason. The federal government imposes a head tax of $50 on Chinese immigrants.
1887	Charles returns to Canada and is appointed minister of finance while still high commissioner.	
1888	Charles resigns as finance minister and moves back to London.	The Fisheries Treaty is passed. The first election takes place in the Northwest Territories.

Even more on the life and times of Sir Charles Tupper

YEAR	CHARLES'S LIFE	EVENTS IN CANADA AND THE WORLD
1890		The Manitoba School Act is passed.
1891		Sir John A. Macdonald dies while in office. John Abbott becomes the third prime minister of Canada.
1892		Sir John Sparrow David Thompson becomes the fourth prime minister of Canada.
1894		Sir Mackenzie Bowell becomes the fifth prime minister of Canada.
1896	Charles becomes the sixth prime minister of Canada (May 1–July 8, 1896).	
1897	Charles retires as the high commissioner to Great Britain.	The Klondike gold rush occurs. Clara Brett Martin becomes the first woman admitted to the bar of Ontario. Queen Victoria celebrates her diamond (60th) jubilee.
1898		The Yukon Territory is formed. The Spanish-American War takes place: Spain loses control over Cuba, Puerto Rico, the Philippine islands, Guam, and other islands.
1899	Charles is defeated in his last federal election.	The South African War (Boer War) begins (1899–1902): The British win control of what is now the Republic of South Africa. The first Canadian troops are sent to the South African War.
1900		The head tax on Chinese immigrants is raised to $100.
1901	Charles retires as leader of the Conservative party. He moves to London, England.	Queen Victoria dies.
1903		The Chinese head tax is raised to $500—the equivalent of two years of labour.
1904		The Trans-Siberian Railway (1891–1904) is completed.
1905		Alberta and Saskatchewan become provinces. The Russian Revolution occurs: Russians protest against the government of Czar Nicholas II.
1908	Charles joins the Privy Council of Great Britain.	
1909	Charles retires to The Mount in Bexleyheath, near London.	
1911		Sir Robert Laird Borden becomes the eighth prime minister of Canada (1911–1920).
1912	Charles's wife, Frances, dies.	
1914		Canada declares war on Germany in September. The War Measures Act is passed. World War I (1914–1918) begins on August 1.
1915	Charles dies in his sleep on October 29.	The first major battle is fought by Canadians during World War I. Known as the Battle of Ypres, in Belgium, it lasts from April 22 to May 25.

Glossary: words and facts you might want to know

Aberdeen, Lady (1857–1939): born Ishbel Maria Marjoribanks, she was the wife of Lord Aberdeen, who was governor general of Canada from 1893 to 1898. She was active in the struggle to increase women's rights in society. While in Canada, Lady Aberdeen founded the Victorian Order of Nurses and helped form the National Council of Women, of which she was the first president.

Aberdeen, Lord (1847–1934): seventh governor general of Canada (1893–1898). Born John Campbell Hamilton Gordon in Edinburgh, Scotland, he moved to Canada for the time that he was governor general.

anthrax: a highly fatal disease caused by bacteria called *bacillus anthracis*. It can affect all mammals, including humans. In cattle, the time between noticing symptoms and death can be just several hours.

Big Bear (1825–1888): Ojibwe/Cree leader of First Nations peoples in what is now Saskatchewan. He wanted to gather his people onto a massive reserve rather than small, scattered ones as the Canadian government preferred. He only signed a treaty in 1876 to sell his people's land when they were starving because the buffalo had disappeared. When life on the reserve did not improve, young men in his band attacked villages and Hudson's Bay outposts during the Northwest Rebellion of 1885. Big Bear surrendered and was sentenced to jail for three years.

Borden, Sir Robert (1854–1937): defeated Sir Wilfrid Laurier and the Liberals to become Canada's eighth prime minister (1911–1920). He was born in Nova Scotia and worked as a teacher before becoming a lawyer. He entered politics in 1896 as a member of the Conservative party.

Bowell, Sir Mackenzie (1823–1917): Canada's fifth prime minister (December 12, 1894–April 27, 1896). His short term included trying to re-establish the Catholic separate-school system in Manitoba in 1895.

British North America (BNA) Act: law passed in 1867 that united the Province of Canada (made up of Canada East and West), Nova Scotia, and New Brunswick into the self-governing Dominion of Canada. It created the federal and provincial systems of government and set the rules for how they share the power to govern the country.

cabinet minister: a member of the legislature (House of Commons or Senate) who has been invited by the prime minister to head a major government department or ministry of state. The cabinet acts as a unit; any opinion expressed by a minister is that of the whole cabinet.

Canadian Constitution: the set of highest laws (or rules) in Canada that dictate how the government is supposed to govern the country. It first became law in 1867 in Great Britain.

Canadian Medical Association: an organization of doctors that formed in 1867 to standardize the quality of members in the profession. It also acts as the voice of all doctors in Canada. Charles Tupper was its first president, a position he held for three years.

Canadian Pacific Railway: the first railway to cross Canada from coast to coast. Construction began in 1882. By the end of 1885, the tracks ran from Montreal to the Pacific coast. In 1889, the railway became truly transcontinental after tracks were laid through Maine to Saint John, New Brunswick.

Cartier, George-Étienne (1814–1873): a lawyer and politician from Lower Canada, he was co-premier of the Province of Canada with John A. Macdonald from Upper Canada (1857–62). He was Macdonald's ally in trying to unite the British North American colonies and was a Father of Confederation. He also served as Canada's first defence minister and often replaced Macdonald as prime minister and leader of the government in the House of Commons.

Cartier, Jacques (1491–1557): a French explorer of the St. Lawrence River to present-day Montreal. He was actually trying to find a shortcut to China. He made three voyages to North America in 1534, 1535, and 1541.

chief medical officer: a qualified medical doctor whose duties do not include treating individual patients but rather advising about public-health matters. Some activities include creating programs to prevent illnesses (like asthma) or the spread of illnesses (like influenza).

colonies: groups of people living in a new territory who are governed by the laws of a mother country. For example, Upper and Lower Canada were colonies of England.

For more information on the terms listed in this glossary, visit www.jackfruitpress.com

More words and facts you might want to know

Confederation: the union of states or provinces to form a new country.

Conservative Party of Canada: the first party to govern the Dominion of Canada. It began in 1854 when politicians from Canada East and West joined to form a coalition government for the Province of Canada. It was initially called the Liberal-Conservative party but changed its name to the Conservative party when a separate Liberal party was formed at the time of Confederation. Sir John A. Macdonald was its first leader.

dowry: a gift of money, land, or valuables given by a bride's family to the groom. It was seen as her family's contribution to the household expenses.

Fathers of Confederation: all of the people who represented the British North American colonies at one or more of the three conferences that paved the way for the Canadian Confederation. The conferences were held in Charlottetown, Quebec, and London, England between 1864 and 1867. Thirty-six parliamentary delegates attended one or more of them.

Fenians: or Fenian Brotherhood, a radical group of Irish immigrants in the United States. Members wanted to invade the British colonies and take control of them. Their plan was to return the colonies to Great Britain once it had granted control of Ireland back to the Irish. In 1866 and 1870, they conducted unsuccessful raids into Canada East and West.

governor general: the representative of the British Queen or King in Canada who provides the royal assent necessary for all laws passed by Parliament. The governor general is a figurehead who performs only symbolic, formal, ceremonial, and cultural duties, and whose job is to encourage Canadian excellence, identity, unity, and leadership. Governors general are Canadian citizens appointed for terms of approximately five years. During their terms, they live and work in the official residence of Rideau Hall in Ottawa, parts of which are open to the public as an historic site, art gallery, and educational centre.

high commissioner: senior diplomat from one country who acts as a high-ranking representative in another country.

House of Commons: the lower house of Parliament. It consists of a speaker, the prime minister and his cabinet, members of the governing party, members of the opposition parties, and sometimes a few independent members (elected members who do not belong to an official party). The members of the House (called members of Parliament or MPs) are elected in constituency elections or by-elections by the Canadian people. The House (often incorrectly referred to as Parliament) is important because it is where all new laws start.

Howe, Joseph (1804–1873): premier of Nova Scotia (1860–1863). Born in Halifax, Joseph was a controversial journalist before entering politics. He led the opposition forces against Confederation.

Hudson's Bay Company: the business that was incorporated in England in 1670 to trade fur with First Nations peoples and control all lands whose rivers and streams drained into Hudson Bay. This huge area, called Rupert's Land, stretched from Labrador, across modern-day Quebec and Ontario, to south of the present United States/Canada border and west to the Canadian Rocky Mountains. In 1870, the HBC sold most of Rupert's Land to the Canadian government. The company evolved into the chain of retail stores now known as "The Bay."

Johnston, James William (1792–1893): premier of the colony of Nova Scotia (1844–1848, 1857–1859, 1863–1864). A lawyer by training, he played a major role in ending the coal monopoly in Nova Scotia, where, until 1857, one company controlled all the coal production in the colony. He passed leadership of the Conservative party to Charles Tupper when he was promoted to be a judge in 1864.

Laurier, Sir Wilfrid (1841–1911): Canada's seventh prime minister and the first one who was a French Canadian.

Liberal party: political party that adopted its name in 1867, after Confederation. It was formed from the union of the pre-Confederation Reform party (of what is now Ontario) and Parti rouge (in present-day Quebec).

Lower Canada (1791–1840): province created by the Constitutional Act of 1791, which divided the former Province of Quebec into two parts: Upper Canada and Lower Canada. These two

Glossary: words and facts you might want to know

provinces were joined once again to form the Province of Canada in 1841 and were also known as Canada West (later Ontario) and Canada East (later Quebec).

Macdonald, Sir John A. (1815–1891): Canada's first prime minister (1867–1873, 1878–1891). Born in Scotland, he moved to Upper Canada with his family in 1820. He trained and worked as a lawyer before becoming involved in politics. He spent many years working to bring the Province of Canada and the Maritime provinces together. On July 1, 1867, his dream came true with the creation of the Dominion of Canada.

Macdonald, Susan Agnes Bernard (1836–1920): second wife of Sir John A. Macdonald. They married in February 1867 and had one daughter together, Margaret Mary Theodora. She and Mary moved to England after John's death in 1871. She died there and was buried in the Ocklynge Cemetery in Eastbourne, a city south of London.

McDougall, William (1822–1905): as minister of public works in Sir John A. Macdonald's cabinet, he organized the purchase of Rupert's Land from the Hudson's Bay Company. In 1869, he was appointed lieutenant-governor of the Northwest Territories but he was prevented from entering by Louis Riel's men.

McGee, Thomas D'Arcy (1825–1868): journalist, poet, and politician born in Ireland. He was elected to the Legislative Assembly of the Province of Canada (1857–1967) and was a Father of Confederation. He was also a member of the first Canadian Parliament following Confederation. In his younger years, he believed that Ireland should be free of Great Britain's control. His later criticism of the Irish-independence movement and the Fenians may have resulted in his assassination.

Manitoba Schools Question: the debate about whether Manitoba should have publicly funded Catholic schools in addition to its non-denominational (non-religious) public schools. When the province formed in 1870, both types of schools were paid for by public money. In 1890, the provincial government ended support of the Catholic schools. The federal government had the power to restore the schools but could not find a solution for many years.

Maritimes: region on the Atlantic coast of Canada that includes the provinces of Nova Scotia, Prince Edward Island, and New Brunswick.

Medical Society of Nova Scotia: association of doctors in the province of Nova Scotia. Founded in 1854, it registers and licenses doctors to practise in the province.

member of Parliament (MP): politician who is elected to sit in the House of Commons. During a general election, the country is divided up into ridings (or constituencies). Voters in each riding elect one candidate to represent them in the government as their MP.

Métis: a person whose ancestry is half First Nations and half French Canadian. Métis culture combines both backgrounds.

Morse, Frances Amelia (1826–1912): born in Amherst, Nova Scotia, she became Charles Tupper's wife in 1846. They had three sons and three daughters.

Northwest Rebellion (1885): the second rebellion led by Louis Riel. By the 1880s, European and other settlers were moving into what is now Saskatchewan; the Métis saw their lifestyle threatened. First Nations people had signed treaties giving up claim to the territory and agreed to settle on reserves. The Canadian government, however, didn't live up to its end of the deal. The Métis of Saskatchewan invited Riel to help them. He set up a government, but it was overthrown by Canadian soldiers. Riel surrendered and was hanged for treason.

potato famine: the widespread loss of the potato crops in Ireland and western Europe, in 1845, 1846, and 1848. This was due to a blight, or fungus, that turned the potatoes into inedible black and soggy lumps in the ground. It was such a disaster in Ireland because potatoes were the main source of food for most people. Some 500,000 to one-million people died of starvation. Another million-and-a-half Irish moved to Great Britain, Canada, the United States, and Australia to escape the famine.

Poundmaker (1842–1886): Plains Cree chief in what is now Saskatchewan. His band was starving because the buffalo were disappearing. He insisted that the federal government supply food and farm tools so that they could become farmers. When government promises were not kept, his band members wanted to join the

More words and facts you might want to know

Northwest Rebellion. He surrendered when the uprising was over and spent three years in jail.

provincial secretary: a senior position in the pre-Confederation colonial and post-Confederation provincial governments until it was abolished by all provinces but Saskatchewan. In Nova Scotia, the provincial secretary was the treasurer of the province and took care of official communications with the Colonial Office in London and other provincial and colonial governments (and, after 1867, the federal government). The position also included welcoming visiting dignitaries.

quarantine: the isolation for a certain period of time of a person or living organism (including animals, plants, agricultural products, and micro-organisms) that may be carrying an infectious disease. This allows time for testing and for disease symptoms to appear, if the person or organism is infected. The introduction of diseases or pests into an area can then be prevented.

Red River Rebellion (1869–70): the events in which the Métis and other residents of Red River (now southern Manitoba) took up arms against the Canadian government. The crisis arose when the Hudson's Bay Company agreed to sell Rupert's Land, which included Red River, to Canada. In protest, Louis Riel and other Métis set up a provisional government to negotiate with Canada. Things turned violent when some Canadian settlers took up arms against the Métis. The Canadian government responded by sending troops to enforce federal authority. Riel fled before the expedition arrived and

went into exile in the United States. The Canadian government eventually agreed to meet some of the demands of the Métis. The result was the Manitoba Act, which created the province of Manitoba.

Riel, Louis (1844–1885): a Métis lawyer who led two armed rebellions against the Canadian government to defend the rights and lands of the French and First Nations people in the territories that later became Manitoba and Saskatchewan. Riel led the Red River Rebellion in 1869, then went into exile in the United States, fearing for his safety. He later moved to Saskatchewan, where he led the Northwest Rebellion in 1885. This rebellion was quickly crushed and Riel was hanged for treason.

Senate: the upper house of Parliament. Here, senators examine and revise legislation from the House of Commons (the lower house of Parliament), investigate national issues, and represent regional, provincial, and minority interests. The Senate can also introduce its own bills.

Stewart, Alexander: uncle of Sir Charles Tupper's wife, Frances Morse. He was a lawyer who served as representative of Cumberland County in the Nova Scotia House of Assembly (1826–1838). He was later appointed a judge.

Thompson, Sir John Sparrow David (1845–1894): Canada's fourth prime minister and the first Roman Catholic one. He helped create Canada's first criminal code, which gave the federal government the power to prosecute criminal offences.

Tupper, Sir Charles Hibbert (1855–1927): second son of Sir Charles Tupper, he became a Conservative MP and sat in the House of Commons for 22 years.

Upper Canada (1791–1841): province created by the Constitutional Act of 1791, which divided the former Province of Quebec into two parts: Upper Canada and Lower Canada. These two provinces were joined once again to form the Province of Canada in 1841 and were also known as Canada West (later Ontario) and Canada East (later Quebec).

US Civil War (1861–1865): war fought between the northern states of the United States and the southern states that demanded to separate from them. The issues were slavery, trade and tariffs, and the rights of the states.

Washington Treaty: in effect from 1873, an agreement between Great Britain and the United States that gave US fishermen access to Canadian fishing grounds for 12 years in exchange for $5,500,000. Canadian companies were also given permission to sell their fish in the US market.

World War I (1914–1918): also known as the First World War, or the Great War. It was an international conflict that involved most of the countries of Europe as well as Russia, the United States, and other regions. The war pitted the Central Powers—mainly Germany, Austria-Hungary, and Turkey—against the Allies—mainly France, Great Britain (including Canada), Russia, Italy, Japan, and, from 1917, the United States. It ended with the defeat of the Central Powers.

For more information on the terms listed in this glossary, visit www.jackfruitpress.com

Index

CONVENTION AT CHARLOTTETOWN, PRINCE EDWARD ISLAND,
OF DELEGATES FROM THE LEGISLATURES OF CANADA, NEW BRUNSWICK, NOVA SCOTIA, AND PRINCE EDWARD ISLAND, TO TAKE INTO CONSIDERATION THE UNION OF THE BRITISH NORTH AMERICAN COLONIES.—SEPTEMBER 1, 1864.

Is this a great country or what?

We've got the Rockies, the Mounties,
the Prairies, and the Barenaked Ladies.

And how about those Prime Ministers?
In their own way, they're a natural wonder too.
Each one as different as a snowflake...

Some of them made us laugh,
some made us cringe.
Others even made us furious.

Get to know each one.
One at a time.
Warts and all.